She Loo
Of My Face

Christine Bousfield

Indigo Dreams Publishing

First Edition: She Looks Out Of My Face
First published in Great Britain in 2011 by:
Indigo Dreams Publishing
132 Hinckley Road
Stoney Stanton
Leicestershire
LE9 4LN

www.indigodreams.co.uk

ISBN 978-1-907401-53-4
British Library Cataloguing in Publication Data. A CIP record for this book can be obtained from the British Library.

Designed and typeset in Palatino Linotype by Indigo Dreams.

Cover design by Ronnie Goodyer at Indigo Dreams.

Printed and bound in Great Britain by Imprint Academic, Exeter.

'Everything in the sphere of this first attachment to the mother seemed to me ...so grey with age and shadowy...that it was as if it had succumbed to an especially inexorable repression.'

Sigmund Freud

'The psychical apparatus is caught in the double vectorization tending now towards the future, now towards the past, in the pure present of dreaming.'

André Green

Introduction by Helen Clare

"It's all down to Constitution." And so it is. Poetry is made from the breath and beats of the body. It holds in its cadences the strengths and flaws of the body, the burdens of gender and of age. It is of place: as much as the body is built from the air and the water around us, so a poetic voice derives from the voices we have imbibed, willingly or not, from emphases and expressions which themselves were born in the exertions required to wrest a living from the land or from the industry imposed on it.

Coming from the other side of the hills, when I first read Christine's work I was struck by how "Yorkshire" it was. Partly, I think, it's the dipping inflection I hear as I read many of the final lines, the last breath of the poem let out with a sardonic twist that either underpins or undermines the rest of the poem. Sometimes it's a hint of the vernacular; sometimes it's the way a line break drops into a phrase that's unassumingly iambic.

This is also, to my ear, an undeniably female voice. It has much in common with the voices I grew up with, those quieter voices that came without bluster or bravado and were all the more insistent because of it.

These are poems rooted in the experience of being female and of inhabiting the female body. They are poems which challenge shame, which accept the responsibility for the generations, which examine without sentimentality the experience of motherhood and of being a grandparent, and confront with honesty, humour, and occasional incredulity, the indignities of ill-health and ageing.

They are poems of place too, from the small houses with fireless grates to Sunday parks and days at the seaside to rivers, sloping gardens and the view of the moors.

And despite their sometimes dark subject matter, they are poems which manage to maintain that most Northern of virtues, cheerfulness, from time to time bursting into joy, becoming transcendent.

Helen Clare, May 2011.

Acknowledgements

'**Epitaph**' *Envoi*, 151, 2008.

'**Mother**' *Pennine Poets Anthology Skylights*, p7-8; *Forty Years of Pennine Poets: Mind and Body 2006.*

'**Voices in the Back-street**' *Aesthetica, A Review of Contemporary Artists,* Issue 11, 2005.

'**Wake**' *The North 37,* November 2005.

'**Woman Drew a Muscle From Between Her First and Second Ribs** *Cinnamon Finalists' Anthology Sometimes,* 2006.

'**The Hare**' *Pennine Poets Anthology Skylights, 2002; Forty Years of Pennine Poets, Mind and Body; Aesthetica, A Review of Contemporary Artists,* Issue 9, 2005; *Cinnamon Finalists' Anthology Sometimes,* 2006; *WriteOutLoud Poem of the Month* chosen by Gaia Holmes, June 2008.

'**Firstborn**' *Perceptions 42,* Winter, 1998.

'**Intensive Care**' *Pennine Platform,* Vols. 51-2, September 2002; *Images of Women,* Arrowhead; *Cinnamon Finalists' Anthology The Ground Beneath Her Feet, 2008.*

'**Wizard**' *Dreamcatcher 13,* Spring 2004.

'**Foxtrot**' and '**Dirty Linen**' *Journeys Anthology* for A Mind Odyssey, Leeds, June 2002.

'**Dirty Linen**' *The Beehive Poets Anthology, Bradford, 2003* (ed. Geoff Hattersley).

'**Foxtrot**' *Praesepia, 2006.*

'**Catherine**' *Swarm, Beehive Anthology, 2008.*

'**Wallpaper**' *The Beehive Anthology, 2003* (ed. Geoff Hattersley).

'**Why Risk Your Arm With A Greedy Lover**' *The Beehive Anthology (ed. Geoff Hattersley),2003.*

'**Minimed 508 Insulin Pump**' *The Iron Anthology of Humorous Verse, 2010.*

'**Curtains**' *Cinnamon Finalists' Anthology The Ground Beneath Her Feet, 2008; The Once Orange Badge Supplement Issue 6,* December 2005.

'**Let Age...**' *Nightingale* emagazine 2002; and in The *Beehive Anthology Swarm* 2008.

'**Strawberries for Jude**' *Perceptions* 43, Spring,1999, *The Weekend Poem BBC Knowledge Text* 18th-20th May 2001.

'**Brothers**' Cinnamon Press anthology *Only Connect, 2007.*

'**Him**' *Dream Catcher 17,* 2006.

'**New Year**' *Orbis* Issue 35, February 2006.

'**Disclosure**' *Envoi,* 151, 2008.

'**False Connections**' *YACYAC Yorkshire Arts Circus Literary Magazine* Issue 1, July 2005.

'**Song**' written with composer Emma Nielsen, performed at the Royal Northern College of Music, March 2008 and at *Leeds Lieder Festival,* October 2007, by Andrew Dunlop (pianist) and Carolina Krogius (mezzo soprano).

'**Advice for Depressives**' Envoi 151, 2008.

'**Baildon Moor**' *Cinnamon Press Anthology Only Connect, 2007.*

'**Hope**' *Enigma* magazine and *Soul Feathers*, an anthology of poetry for Macmillan Cancer.

'**Waiting for Ella**' *Envoi* 150th Gala Issue, 2008.

'**Old Friends**', '**To God, as a Quantum Riddler**' and '**Von Englein Bewacht**' in Christine Bousfield, *Cutting a Rhythm Out of Nowhere* (Poetry Monthly, 2009).

'**White Out**' *Pennine Platform, Dark Mountain Issue I,* and *Phat'itude, (Magazine for the Intercultural Alliance of Artists and Scholars, New York) Spring 2010.*

I would like to thank Helen Clare, Rommi Smith, Phil Sissons, Carol Satyamurti, Christine Webb, and Gerard Benson for their comments and help.

Note: A number of these poems have been performed by *Nightdiver* Poetry and Jazz at various venues in the UK, and on CD.

CONTENTS

She Looks Out
Of My Face

For all eleven of us, and for those who went before.

EPITAPH

It will kill me in the end, in the end it always does,
washes away silence, swills down hyperbole into foam
between stones. My mother was right, keep your eyes
downcast, on the job. But she turned her eyes away.

Fumin beings in *billages,* the baby says. What a lark,
down the hill with the push-chair at six am, played, loved, all
lost on the rocks of the next generation. Don't let evil enter
your heart, blow it out, or fan the sterilising flames.

Mediate. Blessed are the peacemakers, inheritors of mud,
loneliness a passion of a kind, no poetry here, only in the grim
details of history, dead window-cleaners, the grit
in the oyster; and who wants pearls but swine?

MOTHER I

Swill it up, eyes down. Don't say a thing.
Keep it shut. These are my mother's gifts;
and when someone boasts
or says it's no big deal,
she lifts her eyes heavenward.
One day I'll be like her: it'll be easier.

HYDROPHOBIA

A rum lot those people at Number 8. They drank. Her,
Mackeson for iron from a jug at the side of The Cardigan; him,
Dark Mild with the housekeeping in the Coach and Horses.

He surprised Italians in the Great War drinking wine
by the pint. They regularly got the poker and hearth-brush
to each other in their cups, mostly his when looking for work.

An inheritance of a kind. They had three daughters,
one in the Temperance Movement, Greenhill Chapel,
Leeds Road. Sixty years on my mother likes a drink

with her Lithium. It blots out the years,
the Depression, her arthritis.

VOICES IN THE BACK-STREET

I

She's not been well,
burnt her coat, you know
runs in the family, her grandmother,
locked up after the first world war
when her sons died

but then they all did
no need to take it......

what?

well...........personally

II

Must wash, clean, clean it,
clear it up,
all my fault, really,
this shit, check they've been,
check it's right, up to scratch,
check check
check check

III

She shouldn't have buried her head,
needs to face up to things,
get down to things,
that's the answer.

She gets away with...

with what?

with....... (I don't know)...
murder

II

Must wash, clean, clean it,
clear it up,
all my fault, really,
this shit, check they've been,
check it's right, up to scratch,
check check
check check

IV

Well I've no axe to grind,
nowt to do with me,
brought it on herself,
a free world, you know,
made her bed,
let her lie,
let her lie   and let me

let you what?

let me keep.....(hm)
myself to myself

II

Must wash, clean,
clean it, clear it up
all my fault, really,

this shit, check they've been,
check it's right, up to scratch,
check check
check check

V

It was something I said,
I never found out what
but they took her anyway,
saw her leaving
making as if to speak,
eyes damp cinders now
reflect nothing,
nothing that is but......
but what?

the passing of......
(I suppose)
time.

Chorus

It's all down to constitution,
the genes are cast,
we all die in the end,
and a good thing too,

but it's no way to,
no way to.....

no way to....

Go.

TRAITORS

A photograph, the end of summer, just before back
-to- school days; we're sitting on the stone bridge,
river rushing iron -brown beneath, suds on top.

He squints at the sun, fingers a toy boat, his knees
dimpling between short grey trousers and long socks;
I wear a paintbox cardigan, brown brogues,

my hair side parted flat to the head.
I grin to order. Violence seems unreal
in that sunlight,

a girl with a face and hair like mine
in the supplement this morning,
executed by Stalin the year I was born.

IT WAS ALWAYS SUNDAY

They'd call us to brisket and cabbage smelling of sulphur;
round our kitchen table where small brothers
were circumcised for reasons of hygiene,

we chewed grey string, swallowed to the clatter
of pans, a voice like the hundredweight of coal
delivered down the chute into our cellar.

My place then was a cold front room,
low marble fireplace lit only at Christmas,
my ear to the milky keys

of our piano, or safe in the pen,
my young brother in my arms,
his skin like fledgling feathers.

WAKE
(for my father)

You told me once about a wake lasting three days,
every morning you were roused by voices
drunk with sorrow.

Now I, too, continue to wake and watch,
see your tender eyes brighten in familiar places
and in other faces.

I put aside the horror of that day,
your eyes half-closed, flesh warm,
no breath to answer to a name.

Finally, you looked like a stone priest; the undertaker,
catching my reverent tone, executed the work
accordingly.

Now you are ashes on my tongue
and now I sing
for your sake.

MY MOTHER'S EYES

It's an old song I'm singing. Hers are dark brown,
opaque, where lovers read tender reflections.
Wholesome, Frank said, like eggs and bacon.

What did she see out of the oak-grained frame?
Hopefully not the future, forty years served
for a ruby, flawed from the beginning.

There she stood at the foot of the church steps in parchment
lace, linked to my father, his sepia suit the colour
of her corkscrewing hair. *Anglo-Indian*, he said,

Sallow skin seen many suns. And now her eyes are tired,
mottled with blue, white in the corners got with looking
too hard. Her granddaughter's eyes are like hers,

black lagoons to drown the unwary, remind me
of 'them there eyes', the way they sparkle, trouble.
It never got her anywhere.

ON HIS BIRTHDAY

This year the blossom is unseasonal, trees
take it for snow, toss it back like the ash-gold
shower of her hair.

She wanted you to see the Field of Hope again-
together you watched the flowers stretch
in memory for miles.

The wreath of daffodils she brought from Liverpool
dazzled us amongst the orange, green and purple.

MOTHER II

I'm sorry I never met you, Mother, face to face.
Sounds easy but we hardly ever got it together.
Though you never seemed to notice.

 I'm sorry. We're not supposed to rhyme
with each other, you and me, best work
at maintaining our boundaries.
Which means edges.

Jenny's mother last Sunday in the nursing home,
mouthing her silent screams. We'd better go,
said Jenny and I agreed, get back to the land of the living.

Remember Filey? I ask her as we hurry away.
But what can you say in such circumstances?
Shoot me first, said Jenny.

WOMAN DREW A MUSCLE FROM BETWEEN HER FIRST AND SECOND RIBS

nerve-ends buzzing, fibres twitching,
wrapped it in filo, cooked in her assisted fan,
tested with a sugar thermometer.

'Sweet,' she said, 'forty-five degrees,
he'll walk, not stumble, arms hung loose,
his neck suspended from an invisible arc in the sky,
his voice emerging deep
from my own God-spot,
up the long alimentary corridor,
resonating through the ohhhhh of the uvula,
encompassing histories before and after'.

She took out the little parcel,
stroked it, left it to rise,
still carries the wound with pride.

THE HARE

I'm an arctic ghost, now figure,
now ground, a shiver
on the white horizon;

a fierce and cunning mother,
I bear bone-aching cold,
a tenth of my life each gestation;

teach my young by secret visits
to found their form snug as skin,
each tastes my elixir for five minutes
before I freeze again with the sun.

Yes, I am white as the foot of the Virgin,
eyes set on heaven;
my children, melancholy,
drink my songs in darkness.

But I have two faces, two dances to wrong-foot
the gods. I scurry, a shadow, carrying wild grasses
to those they would see die.

FIRSTBORN

He called me, heaved his feet
first up the canal, clung
to its slimy walls;

swimming in green membranes,
fish fruit whatever, I know him
from the start,
a spark, eggplanted, of light.

NO-BOY

He has dark hair, green eyes perhaps,
his eyes look out wherever I see;

there's more than one of him, an unformed twin,
a lad with history blotted out, an end unknown.

Don't speak of it but gather arms around silence.

MOTHER III

He's in the family grave where she will go,
a grandson with dusky skin, cyanosed, slightly yellow
like her, a post-mortem cut to the head.

There's room for me, she said,
I bought it for five when Father passed away,
not counting your baby. Two hundred pounds.
I didn't think that was bad?

INTENSIVE CARE

Golden girl under the blue light,
small chest rising and falling.
I lift you out of your transparent crib;
you murmur, look at me with a puzzled frown.

I unbutton: you shake your head until
your furious gums lock on. My womb
convulses, remembering we were
two orchids wound upon the same stem.

I thought that like the boy you couldn't live,
felt again his clutching for breath,
but you persisted, held on tight,
tore at my flesh, demanded love.

WIZARD

You always were a bit of a lad: remember when I gave you
eleven quid to buy a warm coat, you came back
with that wizard cape and hat from Leeds?

They sent you home from school for taking
the piss out of the institution, a ridiculous trick,
what kind of mother is she?

But every Christmas, your face bright under red curls,
you leap from corner to corner like fire flashing,
now it's a ukulele, cheapo keyboards hammering all day,

then the double-bass with Grandpa's five hundred got
with fiddle playing, next the recording unit, cu- bass
and all those floppy discs on the never-never.

Later I sing as you cut a rhythm out of nowhere,
you're twenty-eight on Wednesday at three p.m.,
I've bought you yellow Perspex cuff-links with red stars.

FOXTROT

Fox at the bottom of the garden,
eye to eye in the stillness of a land
drained of memory;

behind amber eyes blood moving
in who knows what carnival
whirls of skirts and bodies
rushing to the beat of a red-black fire.

Afterwards, still sitting here in the hissing
heat, I remember how you sped past me
in black-red frills on frills,
taking your sweetness with you,

grass   now   moving
to your irresistible dance.

DIRTY LINEN

She's not like me, socks and knickers
hang out of drawers or lie, a question,
on the floor. I never pick them up.

After she was born I hand-washed
every day, loved the slop of nappies
hauled from the soak,
thudding on the draining board;

woollies itchy with powder, thirsting
after suds, sparkled in the rinse,
chased shrivelling round the spinner.

Outside with the basket, matched pegs
to wriggling babygrows, pinioned arms
and legs of cardies and tights,
wind puffing out her baby creases.

We' re out on the town on Friday night;
she's in platforms, odd socks, crumpled combats,
me a Wallis number she wants but wouldn't wear.
And I want to look like her.

THE SAD SING TOO

Past the old rec shadowing tall trees
where you always played as a kid
and the last malfunctioning gents
of another era,

I think of you, you're dearer than the rest,
they're nothing to you, like old
newspapers settling and striving
in the gutter;

those wild mothers slapping their
butter on a whole loaf, depression
is a serious slackening of economic
activity – I die of it,

fly with it to this darkening street,
your face at the window,
the room lit.

WALLPAPER

When we scraped the seven layers, green, pink and white
took turns behind the radiator, from Laura Ashley
print to hothouse rhododendrons, Sanderson stripes,
dots, checks, subtle or chintzy, falling into ice, ice blue.

They were strangers, their cold rooms forensic
clean, twin beds turned down like bandages
on hidden wounds, their colours kept outside
with the purple clematis, peonies,
dark ivy at the window,
clamouring like unforgiven children.

MOTHER IV

LET AGE…

They happened while sleeping
hieroglyphs on my face;
as the shadows were deepening,
someone else took my place.

Hieroglyphs on my face,
I'm not long for this earth,
someone else took my place,
someone born at my birth.

I'm not long for this earth,
someone else took my place,
someone born at my birth
who looks out of my face.

Someone else took my place,
I fall out of time,
she looks out of my face
and this flesh is not mine.

CATHERINE

As they left they pinned me to the door-frame,
set me grinning, sparking in amber-red and gold,
in case they called in, felt drawn to the hearth,
its glowing coals, its scattering of the cold.

They'll watch. I'll skywrite in loops of fire,
veer off, spin a still point, then corkscrewing down,
extinguish in November leaves by the door
of that strange and secret place called home.

WHY RISK YOUR ARM WITH A GREEDY LOVER?

A toad would love you better,
sit grinning by your side,
hear your murmurs to the wind;

a bear would dance you round
nuzzle your ear, bristle up close,
snuffle the lines in your hand;

spiders would spin you a dream,
hurl you wild-eyed into the night,
leave you in silken bonds;

a snake would swallow its tail,
shed skins to make you shoes,
draw crazed circles in your mind.

No, best give me your arm; I eat well,
don't need to devour the hands I hold.
We two are of a kind.

YOU'RE NEVER MORE THAN TEN YARDS FROM...

Thirty years ago when the sun still shone,
on his third birthday out scuttled the rats
from our septic tank; they were glossy and fat.
Now they remain, all my children are gone

from the house, call me sometimes by phone;
the rats sit at my table, gorge from my plate,
I grow thinner by the hour, and the hour is late.
I'm sewing in stones.

MINIMED 508 INSULIN PUMP

He's my lost twin, my double trouble,
accounts for every whim,
asks me in blinking letters
select? act? program? prime?

sticks to my belly Siamese fashion,
monitors *basal* and *bolus,*
we're supposed to reach synthesis,
my wound's healing over,

I no longer fade between
breakfast and dinner,
shake at three millimols,
snooze at the theatre.

When I press *act* he clicks his answer,
flashes *dual? normal? square?;*
hums a note for each infusion.
Disobey and a wild ketotic Thing waits for me.

So I must add up, record the LCD,
brush out the dust from the reservoir,
check for bubbles larger than
champagne at his pump end or his catheter;

I <u>can</u> take him off for sex if I prefer to.
He's fluorescent blue
with a purple Neoprene jacket.
I got rid of his black leather.

CURTAINS

Tear back the curtains,
roll up the blinds,
let in the light:
there'll be precious little soon.

Let in the light,
long shadows stalk the sun,
less than a glimmer now,
leaves rattle in the drains.

Roll down the blinds
on a sky bloated with rain,
leaden evenings edged with spite.
Quick, close the curtains!

There'll be precious little then
under cataracts of cloud
to keep out the cold,
face down the orange moon.

OLD FRIENDS

At our age we exceed our proper limits,
skin crumpled, crinkled, not quite fitting,
sleep overflowing into day, night waking,

watching, grieving. *Ye are children of the light,*
not dark, improper, diseased. Feed on the past,
airy summer days, jazz picnics in the park,

not milky eyes, dying neurons, gums.
She said she'd crawl through the weeds and nettles
to the river first, her long light hair floating out,

an aging Ophelia. Ouse, stay away from her door,
Aire, last night thundering between your banks, from mine.

STRAWBERRIES FOR JUDE

Hey! Remember the party we had by the river,
rolling chocolate -coated strawberries whole
on the tongue till the shock, the crush,
the red-stained saliva?

you in the water as good as naked, calling come
in, it's cool. You look like an ancient priestess
celebrating Dionysian rites of pure pleasure.

Now we overblown roses knocking on fifty odd
remember our sixties' sowing when love
was the fashion, we wore striped stockings,
laughed at sensible men.

How we joked about age and sadness, said we'd have
zipped- together -wheel-chairs and crocheted hats
to throw in the air on Sunday afternoon seaside excursions,

run amok in Myrtle Park with zimmers,
cheat at bowls. And we forgot the frozen fields,
 the shrivelled buds, the berries of grey-
green that turn to dust with a touch.

Ah, Jude! forget our sad song: our fifty luscious years
upon us, let's idle on the moors or in suburban gardens
after six pm, remembering strawberry days   forever.

MOTHER V

I CAN'T IMAGINE

why he sent you that ankle-length floral culotte set
from Bangkok for your birthday. No, I don't think
it'll shorten. You're seventy-nine, for God's sake.

The turquoise broderie anglaise is a bit girly, don't you think?
And that hat like a wreath planted with pink flowers.
Wouldn't they take you more seriously in cream or black?

And you don't need that purple flammable headscarf
even in this high wind with your ear as it is
and especially when you're lighting your fag
as I push you on Bridlington Prom.

Mother!

BROTHERS

One speaks only by text, a constant bleating,
hands over to his woman when the talk gets tough,
a reputation for saying more than she means.

The second speaks laconically, has given up
on words save expletives with the barman,
one-liners sidled through half-closed lips.

The eldest crackles across the wires emirates
to empire; we speak lost histories, ghostly
conversations snatched from the archives.

Our words are mountain peaks above the sea,
weight and depth beneath; suddenly the flood
rises, drags us into unknown continents,
shattering the land.

HIM

You answered the door to police on the Ripper investigation
fresh from carving a pig for the freezer; they asked you
to leave Nigeria for buying six prostitutes G and T's
in the company bar, striking a blow for liberation.

Under house arrest in Libya you helped Gadaffi irrigate
the desert, slept with a knife under your pillow
even in Bingley, travelled the world with shampoo bottles
and the wherewithal for creating instantaneous Flash!

Left Saudi in the nick of time,
opened a bar in Pattaya,
drank most of the proceeds.

My mother laughs, refuses to worry:
'He'll be back. Have faith,' she says.

NEW YEAR

So many feet under the table,
the cloth dragged down
capsized the family meal,
broken crockery spilling blood.

Wolves prowl the edge of the city,
mind your gates, your gardens.

My mother took her tea home to her tiny hovel,
closed the door to all revenants; dustpan
and brush keep the hearth clean,
her God tame and homely.

Motorbikes roar through sleeping
villages, black lips, pale-faced terror.

Virginia-creeper, leather on vinyl,
good son, godson, let him mad run,
tear up the limbs, crack the hidden
codes, of consanguinity.

Wolves prowl the edge of the city,
mind your gates, your gardens.

It happened to his father, repeat performance,
she swallowed for eyes his mother's
precious stones, tore out the corner sink,
ate his heart alive, woman on the edge looking in.

Motorbikes roar through sleeping
villages, black lips, pale-faced terror.

The sick bear the brunt of generations.
He'd rather die than be imperfect:
her words, he ate them. Now cells
divide, grow teeth and hair.

Wolves prowl the edge of the city,
mind your gates, your hedges.

Wild horse running through the wordscreen,
white flamingo, wings descending,
stone god, eyes swallowing the sky.

PEBBLES AND FLINTS

She should in ground unsanctified have lodg'd
Till the last trumpet; for charitable prayers...
                        William Shakespeare: Hamlet

They interred her in her father's unmarked grave
in Nab Wood: no obituary in *The Keighley News*, too obscure
and contradictory a story to be contained in its columns.

Her casket was decked in pink roses like the hat my mother
wore for her wedding; her sister read Herbert's 'Sweet
and virtuous soul'- it seemed inappropriate.

They didn't bury her at the crossroads at least, over-run by
traffic on the A650; her daughter left a cheap pot lion,
a memento with the ashes, hopes to return next week

with roses. I'm not sure I can find the place. But one day
we'll come back, she'll play a reveille on the school trumpet
he's promised her, after the summer holidays.

DISCLOSURE

I didn't hide in the upstairs room afterwards,
barricade the door or drive onto the moors
where they could follow, find my clenched lips,
call out to me 'Why?' to the end of time.
I told a friend and not from the best of motives.
She passed it on, I was admonished, cured,
wore the scars quietly in my organs. Unlike my sister
who locked herself in, pretended to be sulking
so that only the dogs sought her out, till her daughter
had the police break in, and found the awful thing.

FALSE CONNECTIONS
for G

You can't live with me.
But you can talk to me.
I have words,

girl with my mother's smile, crowded teeth,
dark eyes to drown in, heart
drawn to your dead mother, locked into her rage.

And my brother's face moves over yours
like cloud shadows drifting on sea,
his coal-house grin when a boy of three,
he pulled worms from a bucket at Sandsend.

'I'm not your mother, am I?' I say
to my dying father.
'Aren't you?' he said, hesitating.

MOTHER VI

The shame of dying, of coming home
to that familiar place, looking out of the same face
as my mother, her ordinary face;

the shame of disappearing, a lost monument
grassed over, 'In Memory of my Mother' washed away,
her scattered flowers, broken stones.

SONG

My mother drifts between living and dying.
I dream as I drift between waking and sleeping,
of her as a child   arms clinging round my neck,
both of us falling through the sea.
Je me souviens de ton lait bu jadis[1]

My mother drifts between living and dying.
I hold her hand, she clasps and unclasps it.
I must return, leave her lying in the wreckage,
find my way back, break the surface, fight for land.
Je me souviens de ton lait bu jadis

My mother has finished with living and dying.
I remain in the waves with the storms
and the shadows. The sun is now sinking,
rippling gold in the water. I dream of my daughter.
Je me souviens de ton lait bu jadis

---

[1] Stephane Mallarmé 'Hérodiade' *Oeuvres Complètes*, p47

SNOW

It's snowing now and you lie under it,
whitened beyond all recognition,
cold as your frock, the pink one,
the colour of your shroud.

He came last December, left a Christmas wreath,
scattered grey pebbles near the headstone
naming you, your mother, father,
and my second son, reborn now

in our grandsons. My brother's long gone,
hurtling away from generation, his children,
sister, Mother. Only at Christmas, visits
you with pebbles, wreaths of cyclamen.

GHAZAL IN MEMORY OF JOAN DRUCILLA BY HER DAUGHTER CHRISTINE

She'd buy cardigans from Kirkgate Market
and not in M&S - she 'liked it ordinary';

hated rice except in puddings, and any kind
of cheese but Cheshire, liked it ordinary;

looked Indian on the wedding pictures
in her sister's white sateen- kept it ordinary;

left Dad after the Ruby celebrations,
bought a cottage six feet square, kept it ordinary;

wore her nylon fur to hot June family weddings,
a fag between her fingers, just like ordinary;

made tea for Muslim ladies in the home,
and prayed for all the nurses, just like ordinary;

was plain Joan, despised the name Drucilla.
But her mother had smiled at her second girl,

pronounced her - *extraordinary.*

ADVICE FOR DEPRESSIVES

'Doctors now agree that vigorous outdoor exercise is preferable to
psychotherapy as a prescription for depressed patients.'
Observer, June 12th 2005.

Don't think, don't think, go jogging, swim, scrub the floor,
jump, pole vault, marathon, anything but forget your crimes,
it's all down to Serotonin and genes. So laugh, forget
until you remember. Cry. Picasso's cracked woman.

Let's play that insistent rhythm, Oh Joy, remembering
its first forms, passing through our hands, lovers all, touch
me, taste me to the quick, to the marrow beyond melody,
prosody, blasphemy. *Die Holde Kunst,* is that it? Is that it?

But not enough to hold. Or let silence speak,
that old gossip filling hot balloons.
A rainbow machine in a sunlit window
spinning opals round the kitchen.

BAILDON MOOR

Driving home into clouds grubby like washing
fading on industrial lines;
sudden shifts of smoke and gold, lichen hanging
in rags from dark stone walls, my Clio ready
to take off on the brow of the hill.
Like his Japanese kite on Sundays
dragging him off his feet
and us, running after, laughing.

HOPE

It's the opposite of dead air,
cracking thin dark chocolate
between your teeth, discovering
a berry there; it's the feathery skin of a baby's
neck, a secret voice, rising out of nowhere,
breaking up into glittering tones, giddy rhythms.
It's lemons and butter slowly simmered over boiling water,
apples and cinnamon, new laid eggs, bacon first thing.
And this sudden word on a stone as I walk across the moor,
as if carved into the rose-indigo lines of the sky.

MOTHER AND DAUGHTER I

HIS PORTRAIT

faint breeze   early May
her hair moves   pale blossom
on the damson tree;

shot in perpetual green
two of us   front down   grin
at the Polaroid;

baggy cords   blue jeans
waving   on the washing line
legs in the air.

IN HER SHOES

They're blue and silver padding around her flat,
her purple dressing gown, black socks in the pocket
washed with Kleenex, a card for Jazz UK.

Look down the river as she must each morning
framed in flowers. Be her for a moment,
take on all ills. For her 'all good things'.

WAITING FOR ELLA

April 2004 (tree)
From my window, I can see a tree
like a woman leaning her head to one side,
her hair white blossom.

November 2004 (conception)
Branches
blazing white curls,
damsons follow flowers
folding inwards,
dark seed.

December 2004 (implantation)
I need something stronger than form,
than any known metre, here now
where sweetness has to be, blue veins
on skin, milk rising, sap in the leaves.

Hold hold on to that slimy surface
young god, settle in its fissures,
burrow in blood, ravishment, eternity.

I call you call you metafiction, beginning
of the story, foot, fist, eye, smile, tail,
cling, suck, stay, force space from the cord,
continuous   nourishing.

January 2005 (scan 1)
One gram or two of hope, weight of three four five
paperclips, eyes shut, waxy skin,
the luminescence of two-in-one.

Doppler! keep you safe, beat a long, long life,
more than a speck now, inches, ounces, her joy,
your swingboat rocking, flickering legs and arms,

yellow dots not yet drips suspended in amniotic
surges, you dropping your tail 'raver' ready
to somersault her August   awake!

March 2005 (scan 2)
She sleeps, wakes, a sudden flicker of arms.
Cool child, self-possessed in her uterine armchair,
held whole in papery skin, brain a dark
shadow, smile a possibility.

June 2005 (scan 3)
Serious child   dreaming   on the uterine floor
a Pythagoras   mouthing equation bubbles
into the Amniotic

She floats   beyond   the banded tree-womb
eyes closed   the sweetness   of plums
her lips   cord   belly   uncertain hand

August 1973 (remembering)
I couldn't make her out on the oscilloscope,
searched the shadows for Persephone,
then she broke out, launched by the waters,
shrieking the agony of spring in October.

June 2005 (knitting)
The satisfying click, increasing, purling, looping
the future, slipping one over- a neat raglan. Making up,
filling the gaps, grandmother with gifts
of her labour, her silence.

Cashmere frills for the newborn. To bring her home in,
to hallow broken thresholds. Forgiveness, hope
for good times, heartsease, foxglove, digitalis.

July 2005 (waiting)
A slow hypothesis wrung from silence.
I hold my breath, can't speak this coming,
gradual embodiment, somersaulting
into being, flowering, August fruit.

July 2005 (imminent)
Just to say the plums are ripening in the cupboard,
love coming to fruition. Terror and joy, intransitive,
ineffable. Sit it out, rest, trust the seasons to break
two in one, the opening of flowers, ripening of berries
at the same time, on the same tree.

13th August 2005 (advent)
Just to say, she's come, black hair, spiky, matted,
ripe cheeks, long long legs, nails, fingers like frills.

16th August 2005 (repetition)
I remember the breast pump behind flowered
curtains, you upstairs panting under the blue light.
I shed hot tears of milk cut off from you, your stare
right through me into the future.

And now you're in the kitchen pumping
those tears, that rain. And he with her
in the sunlit living room, the pink roses.

1st September 2005 (Angel monitor[2])
She, sleep soothed, arms flung back above her head,
fists feeling for thumbs. See the curve of her neck,
the ammonite spiral of her ears.

Dozing, dreaming, her eyelids flicker, a trace of slate,
our faces childish drawings on the retina. Here no exercise
of will, just waiting, following the sigh-song of her breathing.

---

[2] An angel monitor 'detects baby's slightest movements and alerts you if
baby goes absolutely still'.

TO GOD, AS A QUANTUM RIDDLER

But I have your measure in the pulse of her dancing feet,
ratio of one foot to the other, the waving grass,
flooding river, green shoots, clouds like clouts of phlegm,

biliousness of a universe that doesn't add up, so awash
with moor and rain, horse chestnut, ash and elder,
dark canopies of leaf staunching a summer sky.

Where a single hawk hangs immobile,
a plane tootles from the left, the river obeying
its own crazed meander, not a hair of a head moving
without that equation, a baby's wisp in the wind.

VON ENGLEIN BEWACHT

My Bobby's in this blueberry, she says, peering
into the fruit. Blueberries are her favourite.
He might be eating a tuna sandwich.
Now she can use the conditional.

It's October. Love- in- a- mist grows straggly and tall
in her garden-I scattered the seeds as an afterthought-
yellow fountains of jasmine spill off the wall,

and the baby crinkles his eyes at the low sun,
smiles reflecting through his bottle, as if
we shared an unspoken, or unspeakable, joke.

THE GARDEN

Lily of the Valley shaking their delicate heads,
Aquilegia moth-thin next to currant bushes,
princesses in red jewels. You try a few for earrings-

they stain your ears and cheeks scarlet.
The snakeshead fritillary, camouflaged
in the tall grasses, watches you with hooded eyes.

Waving from the back is allium,
head bloated, round and purple.
Give him to the nursery bully in the toilets.

Love-in-a mist will be next, spreading her
gentian blue, inviting in the bees
to loll drunk inside her skirts.

Hydrangea's old bonnets of purple and red
will grey to deathheads in December,
leaching the pale snowdrops, narcissus,

bridal crown of Spring. She's best
cut back before Easter. Left until April,
she'll return, raging.

WHITE OUT

No satellites here. Even the old telegraph pole up the hill
is swathed in ivy, hops, waving bindweed,
footed by rhododendron gnawing into its wires.
At night we are pitch black, cut off from

the information highway. Dark matter has gravitational effects,
light, too, draws everything to it like these moths
and ginny spinners banging against my window.

From space, we're a scattering of light across the cold
Northern Hemisphere-we see only stars, collisions
a thousand thousand years old, a history of accidents,

who did what to whom, and in what circumstances,
how best to father and mother an Olympic hurdler,
or a king. But I have no time for celebrities, feel only

the enveloping dark, briar rose petals scattered across
disappearing hills, one rook calling to another in the aspens.

POSTSCRIPT

MY HAPPIEST…

was after giving birth in 1969, the woman in the next bed
warning me you could sleep on a washing line.
And I did. And it's now, when his face is red and blotchy
with crying and the snot runs down onto his top lip
and he looks at me and can't help laughing.
Or when I ask her about pre-school
and she turns up her palms, raises her eyebrows
and shrugs just like our daughter. And, John says, me.

Indigo Dreams Publishing
132, Hinckley Road
Stoney Stanton
Leicestershire
LE9 4LN
www.indigodreams.co.uk

Papers used by Indigo Dreams are recyclable products made from wood grown in
sustainable forests following the guidance of the Forest Stewardship Council.